HANS WILHELM
YOUR CHINESE HOROSCOPE

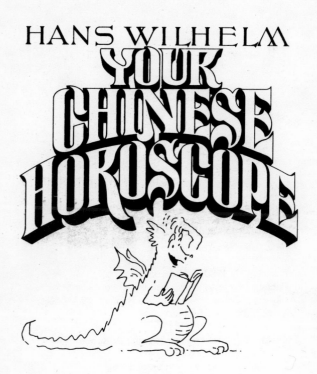

▲ AVON
PUBLISHERS OF BARD, CAMELOT AND DISCUS BOOKS

To my monkey

AVON BOOKS
A division of
The Hearst Corporation
959 Eighth Avenue
New York, New York 10019

Copyright © 1980 by Hans Wilhelm
Published by arrangement with the author
Library of Congress Catalog Card Number: 79-55564
ISBN: 0-380- 75275-1

Cover, title design and handlettering by Richard Nebiolo

First Avon Printing, April, 1980

AVON TRADEMARK REG. U.S. PAT. OFF. AND IN
OTHER COUNTRIES, MARCA REGISTRADA, HECHO EN
U.S.A.

Printed in the U.S.A.

Contents

Your Chinese Horoscope

What predetermines our fate and shapes our make-up?

What motivates our actions and way of life?

What makes us live in harmony with some people and at loggerheads with others? Why do some turn everything they touch to gold while others burn their fingers?

It's no use blaming an unhappy childhood, an alcoholic grandmother, a shabby neighborhood or too early toilet training.

Today we can seek plausible answers in the ancient Chinese mythology, which was for centuries locked behind the Great Wall of China.

The following pages will give a glimpse into the art of divination as pursued in the land of the rising sun.

The guide was inspired by the insights of the Chinese Horoscope.

Like the Western Zodiac, it is comprised of 12 signs. However, unlike the Western Zodiac, the Chinese Horoscope is based on a 12-year rather than a 12-month cycle. Each year is symbolized by the sign of an animal and the individual born under the sign assumes the characteristics, traits and fortunes of that animal.

Since the Chinese year does not accurately correspond to

our calendar year, those born in January or February should consult the chart provided.

Should your date of birth fall at the end or the beginning of the Chinese year you might also come under the influence of the preceding or succeeding sign.

Please remember that the Chinese concept of good and bad in animals does not necessarily follow Western thinking . . . and therefore, be ready for surprises.

WHETHER
YOU ARE A TIGER,
BULL OR
A DRAGON –
DEPENDS ON
YOUR YEAR
OF BIRTH:

January 31, **1900**	– February	18, 1901	RAT
February 19, **1901**	– February	7, 1902	BULL
February 8, **1902**	– January	29, 1903	TIGER
January 30, **1903**	– February	16, 1904	CAT
February 17, **1904**	– February	4, 1905	DRAGON
February 5, **1905**	– January	24, 1906	SNAKE
January 25, **1906**	– February	13, 1907	HORSE
February 14, **1907**	– February	1, 1908	GOAT
February 2, **1908**	– January	21, 1909	MONKEY
January 22, **1909**	– February	9, 1910	ROOSTER
February 10, **1910**	– January	29, 1911	DOG
January 30, **1911**	– February	17, 1912	PIG
February 18, **1912**	– February	6, 1913	RAT
February 7, **1913**	– January	26, 1914	BULL
January 27, **1914**	– February	14, 1915	TIGER
February 15, **1915**	– February	3, 1916	CAT
February 4, **1916**	– January	23, 1917	DRAGON
January 24, **1917**	– February	11, 1918	SNAKE
February 12, **1918**	– January	31, 1919	HORSE
February 1, **1919**	– January	20, 1920	GOAT
January 21, **1920**	– February	7, 1921	MONKEY
February 8, **1921**	– January	27, 1922	ROOSTER
January 28, **1922**	– February	15, 1923	DOG

February 16, **1923** – February	4,	1924	PIG
February 5, **1924** – January	24,	1925	RAT
January 25, **1925** – February	13,	1926	BULL
February 14, **1926** – February	2,	1927	TIGER
February 3, **1927** – January	22,	1928	CAT
January 23, **1928** – February	10,	1929	DRAGON
February 11, **1929** – January	30,	1930	SNAKE
January 31, **1930** – February	17,	1931	HORSE
February 18, **1931** – February	6,	1932	GOAT
February 7, **1932** – January	25,	1933	MONKEY
January 26, **1933** – February	13,	1934	ROOSTER
February 14, **1934** – February	4,	1935	DOG
February 5, **1935** – January	23,	1936	PIG
January 24, **1936** – February	11,	1937	RAT
February 12, **1937** – January	31,	1938	BULL
February 1, **1938** – February	18,	1939	TIGER
February 19, **1939** – February	7,	1940	CAT
February 8, **1940** – January	27,	1941	DRAGON
January 28, **1941** – February	15,	1942	SNAKE
February 16, **1942** – February	4,	1943	HORSE
February 5, **1943** – January	25,	1944	GOAT
January 26, **1944** – February	12,	1945	MONKEY
February 13, **1945** – February	1,	1946	ROOSTER
February 2, **1946** – January	21,	1947	DOG
January 22, **1947** – February	9,	1948	PIG
February 10, **1948** – January	29,	1949	RAT
January 30, **1949** – February	17,	1950	BULL
February 18, **1950** – February	6,	1951	TIGER
February 7, **1951** – January	26,	1952	CAT
January 27, **1952** – February	14,	1953	DRAGON
February 15, **1953** – February	3,	1954	SNAKE
February 4, **1954** – January	23,	1955	HORSE
January 24, **1955** – February	11,	1956	GOAT
February 12, **1956** – January	30,	1957	MONKEY

January 31, **1957**	–	February	18,	1958	ROOSTER
February 19, **1958**	–	February	7,	1959	DOG
February 8, **1959**	–	January	27,	1960	PIG
January 28, **1960**	–	February	15,	1961	RAT
February 16, **1961**	–	February	4,	1962	BULL
February 5, **1962**	–	January	25,	1963	TIGER
January 26, **1963**	–	February	13,	1964	CAT
February 14, **1964**	–	February	2,	1965	DRAGON
February 3, **1965**	–	January	21,	1966	SNAKE
January 22, **1966**	–	February	8,	1967	HORSE
February 9, **1967**	–	January	29,	1968	GOAT
January 30, **1968**	–	February	16,	1969	MONKEY
February 17, **1969**	–	February	5,	1970	ROOSTER
February 6, **1970**	–	January	26,	1971	DOG
January 27, **1971**	–	February	18,	1972	PIG
February 19, **1972**	–	February	2,	1973	RAT
February 3, **1973**	–	January	23,	1974	BULL
January 24, **1974**	–	February	10,	1975	TIGER
February 11, **1975**	–	January	30,	1976	CAT
January 31, **1976**	–	February	17,	1977	DRAGON
February 18, **1977**	–	February	7,	1978	SNAKE
February 8, **1978**	–	January	27,	1979	HORSE
January 28, **1979**	–	February	15,	1980	GOAT
February 16, **1980**	–	February	4,	1981	MONKEY
February 5, **1981**	–	January	24,	1982	ROOSTER
January 25, **1982**	–	February	12,	1983	DOG
February 13, **1983**	–	February	1,	1984	PIG
February 2, **1984**	–	February	19,	1985	RAT
February 20, **1985**	–	February	8,	1986	BULL
February 9, **1986**	–	January	28,	1987	TIGER
January 29, **1987**	–	February	16,	1988	CAT
February 17, **1988**	–	February	5,	1989	DRAGON
February 6, **1989**	–	January	26,	1990	SNAKE

Once upon a time—thousands of years ago—Buddha summoned all animals of the world before him. He promised to reward them well if they obeyed. But, alas, only twelve beasts showed up and Buddha honored them in the order of their appearance by devoting a whole year to each of them.

These were the animals:

The rat, bull, tiger, cat, dragon, snake, horse, goat, monkey, rooster, dog and pig.

Since that time, every man and woman has inherited certain characteristics of the animal which ruled the year of their birth.

The Rat

The Years of the Rat

31 January 1900 to 18 February 1901

18 February 1912 to 6 February 1913

5 February 1924 to 24 January 1925

24 January 1936 to 11 February 1937

10 February 1948 to 29 January 1949

28 February 1960 to 15 February 1961

19 February 1972 to 2 February 1973

2 February 1984 to 19 February 1985

19 February 1996 to 6 February 1997

Clever   Intellectual

Rats are underrated

Seductive

Affable

Playful

Generous

They are elegant by nature.

To keep their wits sharp they love to gamble and have a passion for games, puzzles and the like.

Rats possess business acumen.
The female is particularly resourceful.

Being inveterate hoarders and craving
for snippets they cannot resist
special offers, sales and bargains.

Their life is a constant rat-race.

They thrive on tidbits and scraps of gossip
and therefore are alert and . . .

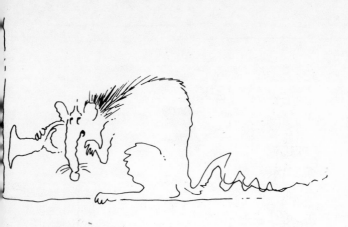

. . . suspicious.

Isolate them with nothing to do
and they would surely die.

Opportunists, they cleverly exploit those around them.

While accumulating worldly possessions . . .

. . . they lavish love and affection . . .

. . . but with ulterior motives.

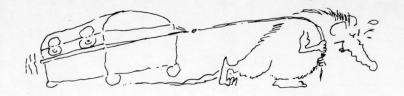

As connoisseurs they appreciate and collect antiques . . .

. . . and objets d'art.

Their aggressive drive . . .

. . . often stirs up trouble and strife.

As excellent hosts they busy
themselves cooking, entertaining . . .

and thus show their flair
for frivolity and fun.

Their light-hearted nature
expresses itself in
unashamed generosity.

The rat gets on best with the dragon, bull and monkey.
Other alternatives would be the pig and the dog.
Totally unsuitable partners for the rat are
the cat and the horse.

To those who have them,
rats are undoubtedly lovable
and pleasurable pets.

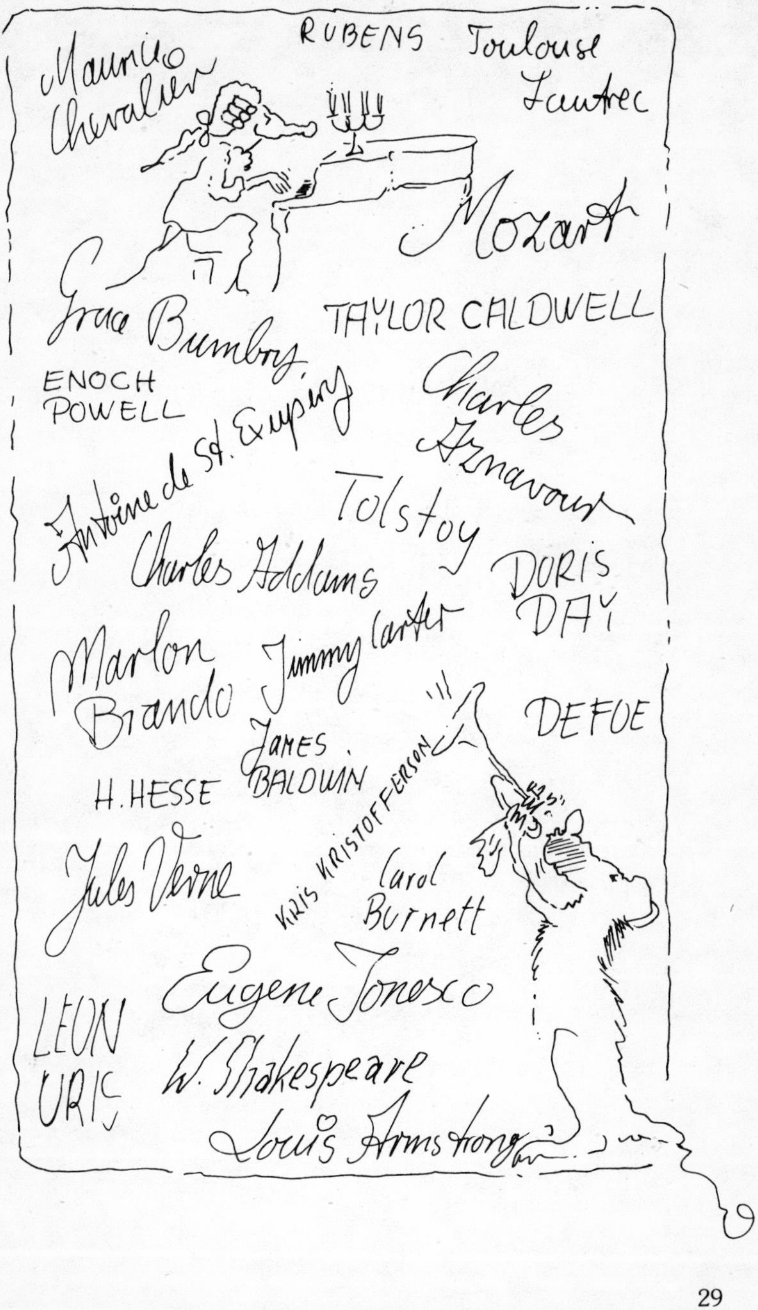
RUBENS
Toulouse Lautrec
Maurice Chevalier
Mozart
Grace Bumbry
TAYLOR CALDWELL
ENOCH POWELL
Antoine de St. Exupéry
Charles Aznavour
Tolstoy
Charles Addams
DORIS DAY
Marlon Brando
Jimmy Carter
DEFOE
JAMES BALDWIN
H. HESSE
KRIS KRISTOFFERSON
Jules Verne
Carol Burnett
Eugene Ionesco
LEON URIS
W. Shakespeare
Louis Armstrong

The Bull

The Years of the Bull

19 February 1901 to 7 February 1902

7 February 1913 to 26 January 1914

25 January 1925 to 13 February 1926

12 February 1937 to 31 January 1938

30 January 1949 to 17 February 1950

16 February 1961 to 4 February 1962

3 February 1973 to 23 January 1974

20 February 1985 to 8 February 1986

7 February 1997 to 27 January 1998

Hard working, strong and down to earth.

Quiet,

enduring . . .

and very methodical.

At times bulls can be a little slow.

Being a conventional and traditional beast,
the bull is not susceptible to new ideas and changes.

Never underestimate
or be fooled by his placid
appearance, for underneath the hide
flows the blood of a choleric;
not afraid of resorting
to violence against anything
that stands in his way.

His pensive mood often
drives him to solitude.

The embodiment of materialism . . .

. . . and authority.

Behind his tough exterior beats a loving heart
capable of bearing long sufferings.

Although the bull is a family type,
unfortunately he is not
known for his romanticism.

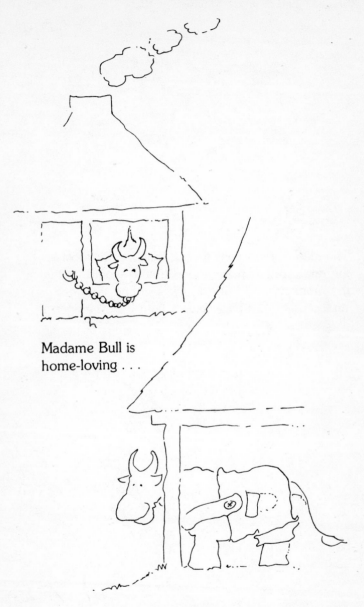

Madame Bull is
home-loving . . .

. . . where she is known to wear the trousers.

The ideal companions for the bull are the rooster,
the rat, and the snake. Good friends would be the cat,
the monkey, and the dog. He will find the goat
unacceptable and will have a fight with the tiger.

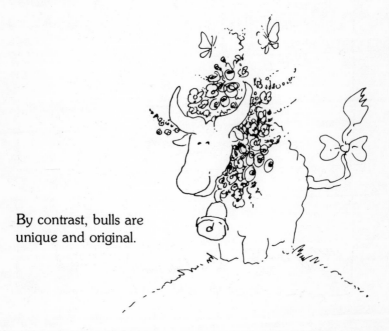

By contrast, bulls are
unique and original.

Vladimir Ashkenazy

HITLER NAPOLEON

DANTE

Lafayette

Louis XIII

Margaret Thatcher

Benjamin Britten NEHRU

RICHARD BURTON TWIGGY

Pierre Boulez

WARREN BEATTY

Robert Redford Marlene Dietrich

ARISTOTLE

VAN GOGH

Shirley

Clemenceau

Timi Lopen Jane Fonda Bassey

Rock Hudson

Renoir

Tony Curtis Perry Como Charlie Chaplin

The Tiger

The Years of the Tiger

8 February 1902 to 29 January 1903

27 January 1914 to 14 February 1915

14 February 1926 to 2 February 1927

1 February 1938 to 18 February 1939

18 February 1950 to 6 February 1951

5 February 1962 to 25 January 1963

24 January 1974 to 10 February 1975

9 February 1986 to 28 January 1987

28 January 1998 to 15 February 1999

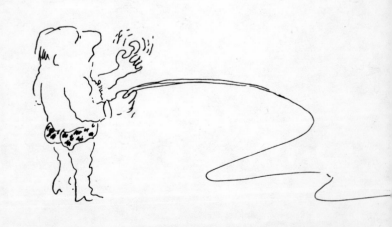

A rebel against authority.

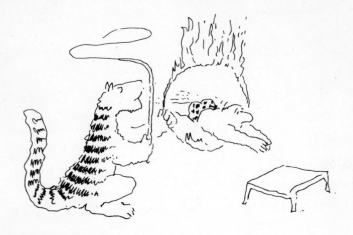

Tigers command respect and subservience
from those that surround him.

They often champion liberal causes.

They are born leaders, . . .

although, they themselves suffer from
bouts of indiscipline, obstinacy . . .

. . . and stubborn hot-headedness.

Tigers display overwhelming generosity . . .

. . . and draw through their irresistable magnetism.

Likeable because of their usually well-mannered behavior—
not altogether free of traces of vanity.

They are in their element while playing
the role of the great protector.

But falling in love with a tiger could prove hazardous.

Tigers get themselves into hazardous situations and live dangerously.

They thrive on and never shy away from risks.

They are typified by their highly sensitive . . .

. . . and quarrelsome nature.

The best match for the tiger is the horse,
the dragon or the dog. But he will also
get on well with the rat and the pig.
The tiger's enemies are the snake,
the cat and, often, even the bull.

Last, but by no means least,
tigers are lusty and passionate lovers.

URSULA ANDRESS

Pierre Balmain

KARL MARX

Charles Lindbergh

Louis XIV

C. DE GAULLE

Isadora Duncan

Evel Knievel

MARCO POLO

Marilyn Monroe

Joan Sutherland

Rudolf Nureyev

L.v. Beethoven

EISENHOWER

Stevie Wonder

Hugh Hefner

TIBERIVS CAESEAR

AYATOLLAH KHOMEINI

The Cat

The Years of the Cat

30 January 1903 to 16 February 1904

15 February 1915 to 3 February 1916

3 February 1927 to 22 January 1928

19 February 1939 to 7 February 1940

7 February 1951 to 26 January 1952

26 January 1963 to 13 February 1964

11 February 1975 to 30 January 1976

29 January 1987 to 16 February 1988

16 February 1999 to 4 February 2000

Cats make super companions

Traditional   delicate   nice

well-bred   tasteful

happy   tender   and peace loving.

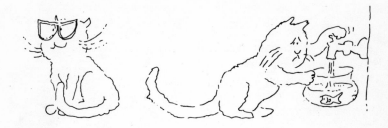

Suggestive of astuteness,   solicitude

and savoir faire.

Sometimes smacking of a certain air of snobbery.

On the other paw, cats can
portray an image of
being superficial, deceitful . . .

. . . rather provincial . . .

. . . and even hypochondriac, . . .

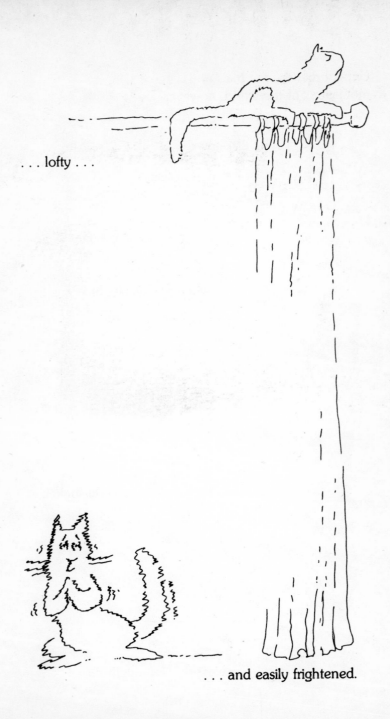

. . . lofty . . .

. . . and easily frightened.

Unperturbed by the trials and
tribulations of the world, however . . .

. . . when personally threatened . . .

. . . then the cat is easily shaken . . .

. . . and spontaneously leaps
onto the tallest tree.

Fortunately cats soon
can be pacified and
are therefore, . . .

. . . quick to forgive and forget.

Although, on the whole, cats are faithful—
for some reason they are not
really made for family life.

By special formula they avoid
confrontations and disputes.

Deeply moved by the problems
and misfortunes of others.

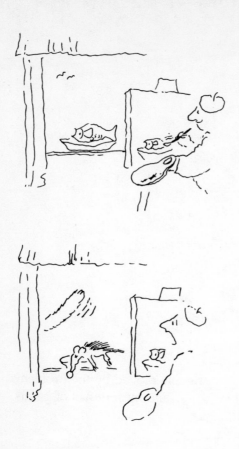

Cat businessmen excel in
typical wheeler-dealer trading.

They make very gentle and
sympathetic bosses whose actions
are governed by strict caution.

Will not shy away from performing
the most menial of jobs—
if so required.

Still, they wish they could
drop out of the madding rat-race.

Cats enjoy their warm, intimate environment . . .

. . . and the friends that surround them.

A good match for the cat is the goat,
the dog, and the pig. Snakes, monkeys
and horses make good partners, too.
But the cat should avoid the rat,
the tiger and the rooster.

Harry Belafonte

Toscanini

BOB HOPE

QUEEN VICTORIA

Curd Jürgens

Peter Fonda.

James Caan

Orson Welles

SiR THOMAS BEECHAM

Arthur Miller

CONFUCIUS

Frank Sinatra

Eva Perón

Anne Boleyn

Marie Antoinette

Albert Einstein

Martin LUTHER

The Dragon

The Years of the Dragon

17 February 1904 to 4 February 1905

4 February 1916 to 23 January 1917

23 January 1928 to 10 February 1929

8 February 1940 to 27 January 1941

27 January 1952 to 14 February 1953

14 February 1964 to 2 February 1965

31 January 1976 to 17 February 1977

17 February 1988 to 5 February 1989

Dragons represent strength, health and good fortune.

Nothing is beyond them . . .

. . . and whatever they do . . .

. . . they perform well . . .

When they set their heart . . .

. . . they even do bad things well.

They do enjoy a show of glitter and sparkle . . .

. . . and certainly impress others
with their own spectacle.

Dragons are athletic types
and through regular exercise
they retain their youthful composure . . .

. . . till a ripe old age.

As born chatter-boxes . . .

. . . they tend to be tactless . . .

but nonetheless, they are quite artistic.

As dragons are rather talkative, they have no difficulty
in communicating with all and sundry.
However, their speech seldom reflects profound thought.

Dragons are not aversed to casual flirtations.

Dragons thrive in splendid isolation
as they are self-sufficient.

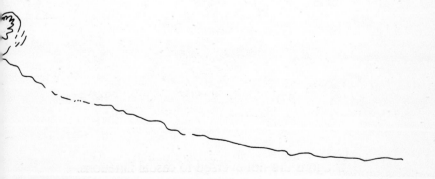

Irrespective of the disaster . . .

. . . that befalls them . . .

. . . luckily for them they end up on top, and are well equipped . . .

. . . to tackle extraordinary situations.

Dragons are idealists and perfectionists.

Dragons often suffer from a sense of superiority.

Despite their appearance of glitter, show and ease,
deep down the dragon is dissatisfied and discontent.

Dragons are happiest on their own or
with a monkey, a snake, a rat or a rooster.
Yet they could also love a tiger or a horse.
However, there will always be a barrier
between them and the dog, as well as the bull.

To cheer-up a dragon—inject a bit of romanticism.

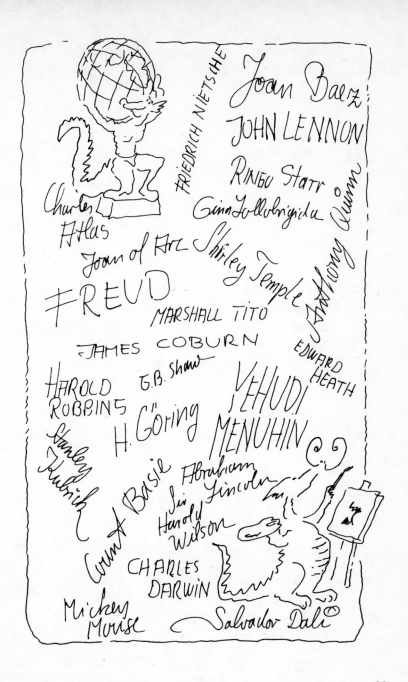

The Snake

The Years of the Snake
5 February 1905 to 24 January 1906
24 January 1917 to 11 February 1918
11 February 1929 to 30 January 1930
28 January 1941 to 15 February 1942
15 February 1953 to 3 February 1954
3 February 1965 to 21 January 1966
18 February 1977 to 7 February 1978
6 February 1989 to 26 January 1990

Snakes are well-bred.

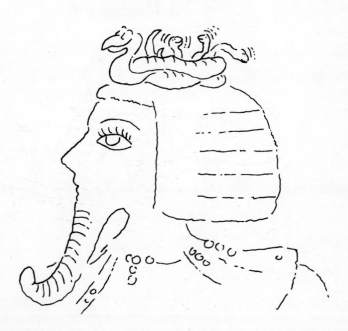

The males are by nature handsome and sleek.

Some betray a touch of snobbery and showy behavior . . .

. . . which sometimes spills over into ostentation.

MONA NAGA

The ladies are captivatingly beautiful and are found to be . . .

attractive and irresistable.

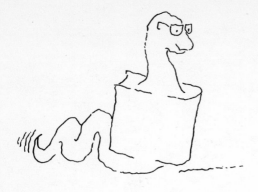

They are highly
thought of because
of their wisdom, . .

. . . gestures
of goodwill . . .

. . . and gentleness.

Endearing for
their sentimental
and romantic
nature and appreciated
for their subtle sense . . .

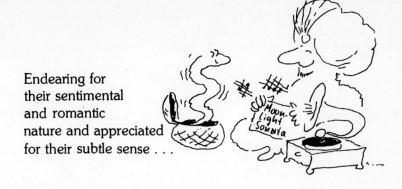

. . . of humor.

Their's is a cultivated taste . . .

. . . and Lady Luck is
well disposed towards them.

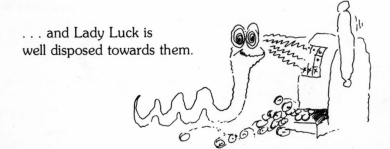

Snakes think widely and deeply . . .

. . . and are extremely self-critical.

Recognized by a calm composure, . . .

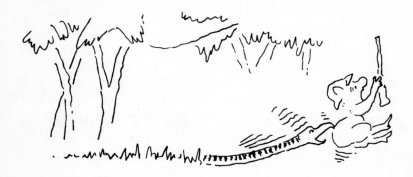

. . . once stirred, they can prove very decisive.

Therefore, try not
to provoke a snake . . .

. . . for invariably . . .

. . . he is a bad
and vicious loser.

Snakes are eager to help, . . .

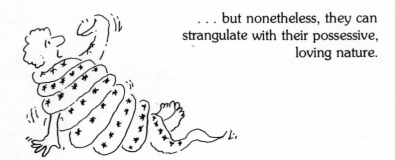

. . . but nonetheless, they can strangulate with their possessive, loving nature.

The grasping snake is driven into many flirtations.

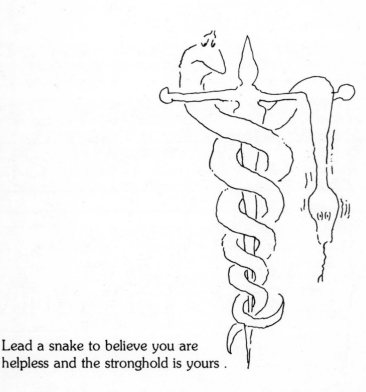

The best match
for a snake is either
the rooster or the bull.
A relationship with a
dragon or a dog could
also work out successfully.
Any affairs with tigers or pigs
are bound to end in misery.

Lead a snake to believe you are
helpless and the stronghold is yours .

Hans Christian Andersen

Grace Kelly

Jacques Brel

J. F. Kennedy

GANDHI

J. P. Sartre

Johannes Brahms

MAO

SCHUBERT

Julie Christie

Goethe

NASSER

Jacqueline Kennedy Onassis

Beverly Sills

Picasso   Miro

The Horse

The Years of the Horse

25 January 1906 to 13 February 1907*

12 February 1918 to 31 January 1919

31 January 1930 to 17 February 1931

16 February 1942 to 4 February 1943

4 February 1954 to 23 January 1955

22 January 1966 to 8 February 1967*

8 February 1978 to 27 January 1979

27 January 1990 to 14 February 1991

*The Years of the Fire Horse

Horses are well-groomed and look terrific.

Not known for their patient disposition . . .

... they tend to tread on other's hooves ...

... and assert ultimate independence.

Egocentric: others, therefore, have to revolve around them.

Inconsistent; they can be hot-headed today . . .

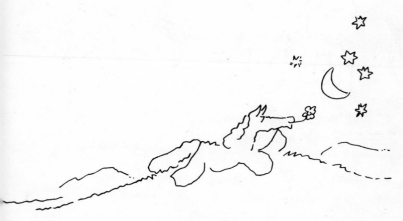

. . . and sentimental and dreaming tomorrow.

The masses find the horse charming, entertaining,
winning, diplomatic, amusing, cunning and popular . . .

. . . and he commands therefore,
their admiration and respect.

Notwithstanding, left to his own devices,
his confidence may melt away.

Horses are home-proud . . .

They have no time for problems
which do not directly concern them.

. . . and value their servants.

They are simple extroverts.

HOW TO TAME A HORSE:

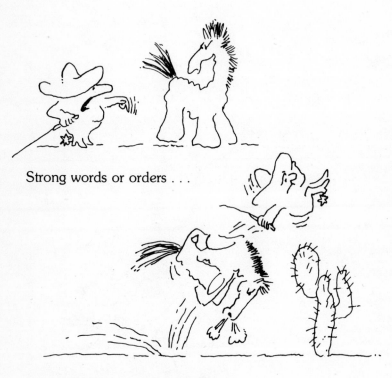

Strong words or orders . . .

. . . rarely have the desired effect.

Ignore the horse, to gain their full attention.

Lavish flattery and admiration . . .

. . . and your's is an easy and smooth ride.

A horse epitomizes sex-appeal . . .

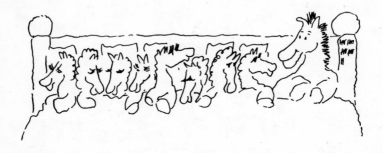

. . . and sensuality.

The ease with which they tackle hurdles
makes them natural champions.

THE FIRE HORSE

A fire horse rises
once in a 60-year cycle
(1906, 1966, 2026 etc.) and
their good and bad attributes are
more pronounced. They tend to go for
extremes and are consumed by their excesses.

A horse should team-up with a goat,
a dog, a tiger or a rooster. The rat,
the pig and the bull might be a bit
too difficult for the horse. But by all means
the horse should stay away from the monkey.

The Goat

The Years of the Goat

14 February 1907 to 1 February 1908

1 February 1919 to 20 February 1920

18 February 1931 to 6 February 1932

5 February 1943 to 25 January 1944

24 January 1955 to 11 February 1956

9 February 1967 to 29 January 1968

28 January 1979 to 15 February 1980

15 February 1991 to 3 February 1992

Goats are for pleasure and therefore,
make good playboys, courtesans and gigolos.

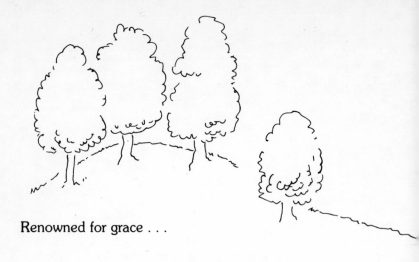

Renowned for grace . . .

. . . and creativity.

They are teasingly playful and amorous.

Often feel gloomy and discontented . . .

. . . believing the grass to be greener
on the other side.

Seeking comfort in religion, . . .

. . . and by contrast, also sheepishly believe
in ESP, astrology and the occult.

Their sense of timing is often lacking . . .

. . . and likewise their sense of ownership is not always defined.

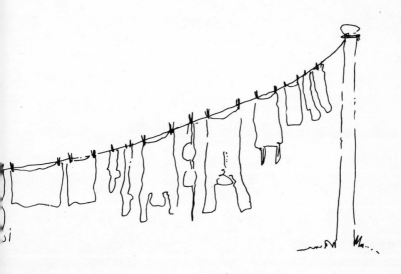

It's a fact, goats are no leaders . . .

. . . but followers.

Goats are ill-advised to enter the world of business.

Well-suited to a lifestyle of luxury
provided by a rich sugar daddy,
successful boy friend or wealthy heiress.

They cherish those who keep them in style.

There is lots of love
in the mind of a goat.

Goats are attracted to the horse,
the pig and the cat. The monkey
could also be the right partner.
But the bull and dog have
little time for the goat.

Coco Chanel

Dino de Laurentiis

Gypsy Rose Lee

Dame Margot Fonteyn

Catherine Deneuve

Anita Ekberg

Herbert von Karajan

Diana Dors

MICHELANGELO

Anne Bancroft

Mick Jagger

Robert de Niro

Rudolf Valentino

John Denver

Liberace

The Monkey

The Years of the Monkey

2 February 1908 to 21 January 1909

21 February 1920 to 7 February 1921

7 February 1932 to 25 January 1933

26 January 1944 to 12 February 1945

12 February 1956 to 30 January 1957

30 January 1968 to 16 February 1969

16 February 1980 to 4 February 1981

4 February 1992 to 22 January 1993

Monkeys are resourceful, amusing and clever.

Monkeys are skillful businessmen.

Can be relied upon to tackle
any complicated problem sensibly.

With infectious enthusiasm, . . .   youthfulness . . .

and expertise . . .

. . . he has the ability to
achieve fame and wealth.

... but often he may resort
to less than conventional ways
of reaching his goal.

Monkeys are ambitious,

vain, . . .

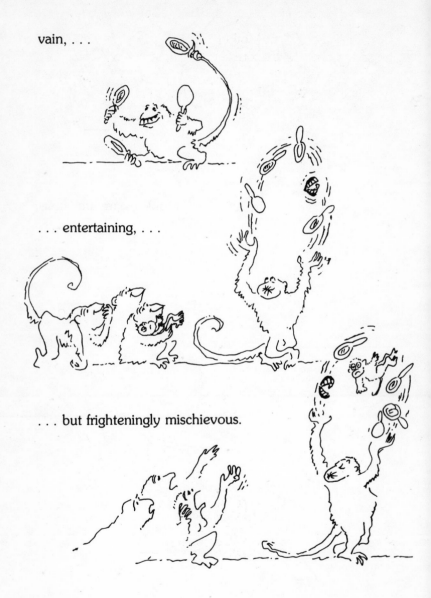

. . . entertaining, . . .

. . . but frighteningly mischievous.

Getting on so well with others
helps to conceal his egoistical
and selfish nature. And in fact,
he has a very low opinion
of those around him.

Yet people always adore monkeys
for their wit, high intelligence and
their keen interest in affairs of the world.

Monkeys are not always truthful . . .

. . . but astute enough not to be found out.

However, not all monkeys are liars . . .

. . . but most liars are monkeys.

Although capable of falling in love easily . . .

. . . love has its pit-falls for them.

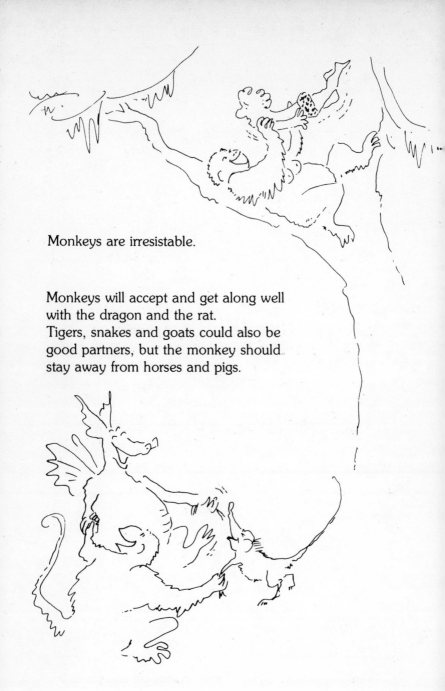

Monkeys are irresistable.

Monkeys will accept and get along well
with the dragon and the rat.
Tigers, snakes and goats could also be
good partners, but the monkey should
stay away from horses and pigs.

The Rooster

The Years of the Rooster

22 January 1909 to 9 February 1910
8 February 1921 to 27 January 1922
26 January 1933 to 13 February 1934
13 February 1945 to 1 February 1946
31 January 1957 to 18 February 1958
17 February 1969 to 5 February 1970
5 February 1981 to 24 January 1982
23 January 1993 to 9 February 1994

Roosters like to eye-catch.

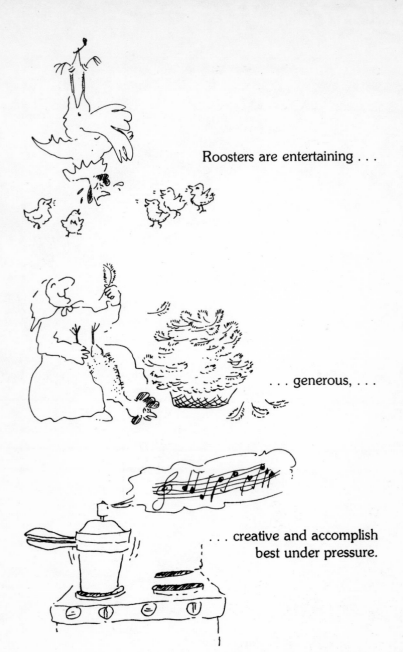

Roosters are entertaining . . .

. . . generous, . . .

. . . creative and accomplish
best under pressure.

They are handsome . . .

. . . and popular.

Soon disenchanted with routine.

Roosters enjoy travel, discovering new horizons
and are keen to try different lifestyles.

Prone to boast and exaggerate.

They are marvelous hosts and
lovers of all kind of species.

Yet, occasional solitude
is essential for them.

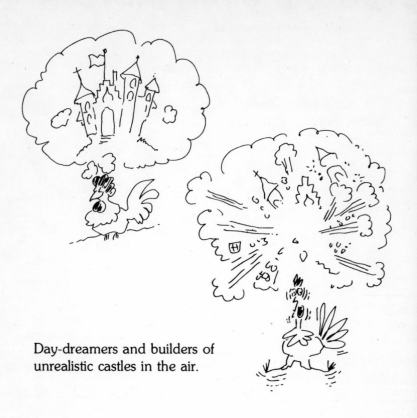

Day-dreamers and builders of unrealistic castles in the air.

The rooster excels in offering
advice and preaching to others.

TONIGHT
sermon
on the
Mount

Their lives are full of ups . . .

. . . and downs.

They are familiar with
bankruptcy and broken hearts . . .

. . . but in the end always
get away with murder.

The rooster gets along perfectly with a bull,
a snake, a horse and a dragon.
But the dog and the rat are also ideal partners.
Naturally he should avoid the cat as well as another rooster.

A rooster needs to be boosted
by unlimited praise.

The Dog

The Years of the Dog

10 February 1910 to 29 January 1911

28 January 1922 to 15 February 1923

14 February 1934 to 4 February 1935

2 February 1946 to 21 January 1947

19 February 1958 to 7 February 1959

6 February 1970 to 26 January 1971

25 January 1982 to 12 February 1983

10 February 1994 to 30 January 1995

The champions for justice and freedom.

Dogs are the Ralph Naders of society.

They are discreet . . .

. . . and helpful.

Extremely generous . . .

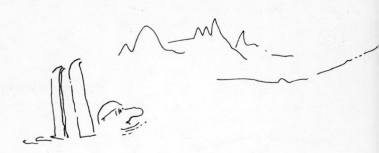

. . . dependable . . .

. . . devoted . . .

. . . dignified,

Respectful, . . .

. . . attentive . . .

. . . and very loyal.

Philosophical, . . .

. . . well-to-do . . .

. . . and bashful.

But they tend also to be the world's
biggest worriers and pessimists.

Introverted, obstinate, and cynical.

When the dog loses his sense
of direction and gets confused . . .

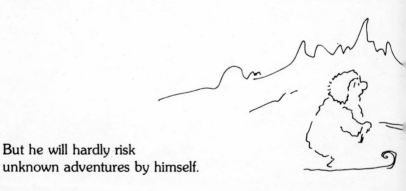

But he will hardly risk
unknown adventures by himself.

. . . he only needs a gentle boost
to set him back on course.

A dog can establish a deep and meaningful
relationship with a horse, a tiger or a cat.
Even the rooster could be
the right partner for him,
but dragons and goats are
a bit too much for him.

You can always count on the reliable dog.

BERTHOLD
BRECHT

Rasputin

Pierre Cardin

Sophia

Loren

Louis XVI

Molière

SOCRATES

Jean Anouilh

G. de Maupassant

Anna
Motto

Jean
Genet

Voltaire

Shirley
Maclaine

W. CHURCHILL

Liza Minelli

The Pig

The Years of the Pig

30 January 1911 to 17 February 1912
16 February 1923 to 4 February 1924
5 February 1935 to 23 January 1936
22 January 1947 to 9 February 1948
8 February 1959 to 27 January 1960
27 January 1971 to 18 February 1972
13 February 1983 to 1 February 1984
31 January 1995 to 18 February 1996

A gallant and courteous friend

Pigs do everything to
please those they love.

It's a shame that they are
so innocent and gullible . . .

. . . bordering on the naive . . .

. . . and therefore, can so easily be cheated.

By nature pigs are peace-loving . . .

. . . and defenseless.

Their character is trustful, honest,
correct, pure, very sincere . . .

. . . and very devoted.

Pigs are usually intellectual.
Discerning in their reading matter.

Pigs sincerely care about others,
but others too often take advantage of that.
Maybe because they are too stubborn to listen.

They are often victims of seduction.

They are very sensitive.
That's why there is so much
sadness in the life of a pig.

To overcome it, they tend to indulge
in all kinds of pleasures. After all, the pig is
a sensualist who knows how to live well.

However, with the right friends to guide
and advise the pig, he could
become unashamedly rich.

The happiest relationship is between
a pig and a cat, maybe a dragon, too.
But the pigs should run away from goats and snakes.

You can really trust a pig.
It will never let you down.

Woody Allen   Henry Kissinger

Fred Astaire

ALFRED
HITCHCOCK   Barbara
Cartland   George
Pompidou

Tennessee Williams   Olivia
Cromwell   CHRISTIAAN BARNARD   William Hearst

BISMARCK

Prince
Rainier of Monaco   KING HUSSEIN

Alain Delon   Johnny Mathis

Albert
Schweitzer   AL CAPONE

E. HEMINGWAY   Elton John